·De Colores·

and Other Latin-American Folk Songs
for Children

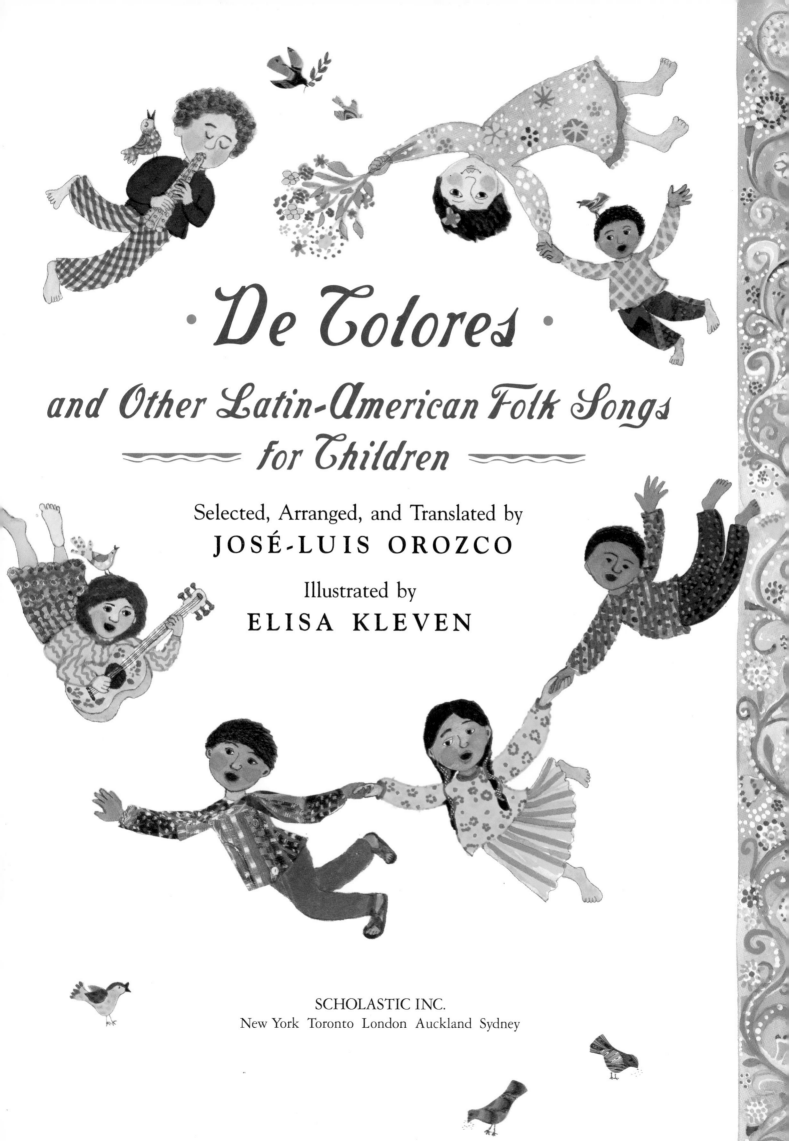

· De Colores ·
and Other Latin-American Folk Songs
for Children

Selected, Arranged, and Translated by
JOSÉ-LUIS OROZCO

Illustrated by
ELISA KLEVEN

SCHOLASTIC INC.
New York Toronto London Auckland Sydney

Para Julie, José-Luis, Maya, Gabriel y Pablito
J.-L.O.

For Sally and her music
E.K.

*The illustrator would like to thank Carol Schneider,
Minerva Mendoza, and the Thomas family
for their generosity.*

ISBN 0-590-03489-8

Published by Scholastic Inc., 555 Broadway, New York, NY 10012,
by arrangement with Dutton Children's Books, a division of Penguin Books USA Inc.

SCHOLASTIC and associated logos are trademarks and/or registered
trademarks of Scholastic Inc.

12 11 10 9 8 7 6 5 4   2 3/0

Printed in the U.S.A.   08

First Scholastic printing, January 1998

The art in this book is mixed-media collage, using watercolors,
pastels, ink, and cut paper.

All of the songs contained in this book have been recorded by José-Luis Orozco
and are available from Arcoiris Records, P.O. Box 7428, Berkeley, CA 94707.

Sing the days of the week in the same manner.

Hoy es lunes, hoy es lunes,
¿cómo estás? ¿cómo estás?
mártes
miércoles
jueves
viernes
sábado
domingo

Today is Monday, *today is Monday,*
How are you? *How are you?*
Tuesday
Wednesday
Thursday
Friday
Saturday
Sunday

cua - tro,   cin - co,   seis,   sie - te   se - ma - nas,

Había una vez
un barco chiquito,   [cantar tres veces]
tan chiquito, tan chiquito,
que no podía navegar.

Pasaron una, dos, tres, cuatro,
cinco, seis, siete semanas,   [cantar tres veces]
y el barquito tan chiquito
que no podía navegar.

Y si la historia no les
parece larga,   [cantar tres veces]
volveremos, volveremos,
volveremos a empezar.

Había una vez...

Oh! once there was
a very little boat   [sing three times]
that was tiny, was so tiny,
that it couldn't sail away.

We counted one and two, three and four,
five and six and seven weeks more,   [sing three times]
and the tiny boat was so tiny
that it couldn't sail away.

And if you think that the
story has an end,   [sing three times]
we are ready, we are ready
to start all over again.

Oh! once there was...

Al tambor · The Drum Song

This song is sung in Panama during carnaval and at other celebrations. The original
rhythm is called tamborcito *and the people of the country are honored:* "Panameña,
panameña, panameña, vida mía..." *In place of the name in the song, sing the name of
each child in a group, one at a time, while she or he plays a small drum or stands up
to dance. Children can also clap hands, snap fingers, or play their laps as drums to the
rhythm of the song.*

quie-ro que tú me lle-ves al tam-bor de la_a-le-grí-a. Al tam-

grí-a, al tam-bor de la_a-le-grí-a

CORO
Al tambor, al tambor,
al tambor de la alegría,
yo quiero que tú me lleves
al tambor de la alegría.
[cantar dos veces]

María, ¡oh! María
María, amiga mía,
yo quiero que tú me lleves
al tambor de la alegría.

CHORUS
Play the drum, play the drum,
play the drum from Panama,
come on let's play the drum
tum, tum, tum, la, la, la, la, la.
[sing twice]

María, Oh! María
María, my dear friend,
it's time to sing and dance
with the drum tum, tum, la, la, la.

Vamos a la mar · Let's Go to the Sea

This song has its origins in Guatemala. Children can also clap hands, snap fingers, click their tongues, or slap thighs in place of the "tun, tun" end-of-line rhythm.

Va-mos a la mar, tun, tun, a co-mer pes-ca-do, tun, tun,

fri-ti-to y a-sa-do, tun, tun, en sar-tén de pa-lo, tun, tun.

Vamos a la mar, tun, tun,
a comer pescado, tun, tun,
fritito y asado, tun, tun,
en sartén de palo, tun, tun.

Vamos a la mar, tun, tun,
a comer pescado, tun, tun,
boca colorada, tun, tun,
en sartén de palo, tun, tun.

Let's go to the sea, tun, tun,
to enjoy the best fish, tun, tun,
eat it fried or grilled, tun, tun,
in a wooden dish, tun, tun.

Let's go to the sea, tun, tun,
to enjoy the best fish, tun, tun,
red-mouthed fish so tasty, tun, tun,
in a wooden dish, tun, tun.

Los elefantes · The Elephant Song

This counting song can also be played as a game. While the group stands in a circle and sings, one child makes the slow-motion sway walk of an elephant inside the circle. At the end of the first verse, the child picks a second child, and both do the slow-motion elephant sway walk. Then the second child picks a third, and so on. This version of the song comes from Argentina.

Un e-le-fan-te se ba-lan-cea-ba so-bre la te-la de u-na a-ra-ña.

Co-mo ve-í-a que re-sis-tí-a fue a lla-mar a o-tro e-le-fan-te.

Un elefante se balanceaba
sobre la tela de una araña.
Como veía que resistía
fue a llamar a otro elefante.

Dos elefantes se balanceaban
sobre la tela de una araña.
Como veían que resistía
fueron a llamar a otro elefante.

Tres elefantes...

One elephant went out to play
out on a spider's web one day.
He had such enormous fun
he called another elephant to play.

Two elephants went out to play
out on a spider's web one day.
They had such enormous fun
they called another elephant to play.

Three elephants...

La granja · The Farm

This song is also sung in other Latin American countries as "Mi rancho" (My Ranch). In Argentina it is called "La chacra" (The Farm). When singing it in a group, it's fun for each child to be a different animal—chick, cow, pig, and so on. When the song calls for the animal sound, the designated child makes it. Then everybody joins in on the chorus and other verses. Notice the way different languages represent different animal noises.

Ven-gan a ver mi gran-ja que es her-mo———sa. Ven-gan a ver mi gran-ja que es her-mo———sa. El pa-ti-to ha-ce a-sí, cuá, cuá. El pa-ti-to ha-ce a-sí, cuá, cuá. Oh, ven-gan, a-mi-gos, ven-gan, a-mi-gos, ven-gan, a-mi-gos, ven-gan. Oh,

ven - gan, a - mi - gos, | ven - gan, a - mi - gos, | ven - gan, a - mi - gos, | ven - gan___

Vengan a ver mi granja	Come to see my farm
que es hermosa. [cantar dos veces]	for it is beautiful. [sing twice]
El patito hace así, cuá, cuá. [dos veces]	**The duck goes like this, quack, quack.** [sing twice]
CORO	CHORUS
Oh, vengan, amigos,	Oh, come, my friends,
vengan, amigos,	Oh, come, my friends,
vengan, amigos, vengan. [cantar dos veces]	Oh, come to see my farm. [sing twice]

Repeat the song, replacing the verse in boldface with one of the following verses.

El pollito hace así, pío, pío.	The chick goes like this, peep, peep.
La vaquita hace así, mú, mú.	The cow goes like this, moo, moo.
El puerquito hace así, oinc, oinc.	The pig goes like this, oink, oink.
El burrito hace así, íja, íja.	The donkey goes like this, hee haw, hee haw.
El gallito hace así, kikiri, kí.	The rooster goes like this, cock-a-doodle-doo.
El perrito hace así, guau, guau.	The dog goes like this, bow wow.
El gatito hace así, miau, miau.	The cat goes like this, meow, meow.

La víbora de la mar · The Sea Serpent

Many versions of this song-game can be found. Two players, children or adults, hold their hands up high to make a bridge or gate. The rest of the players form a line, holding the waist or shoulders of the person in front of them, and weave under the bridge like a sea serpent. On the last line, the bridge makers drop arms, catch a child in the sea-serpent line, and gently rock him or her back and forth. Then the song-game resumes. Several bridges or gates can be made.

A la ví - bo - ra, ví - bo - ra de la mar, de la mar por a -

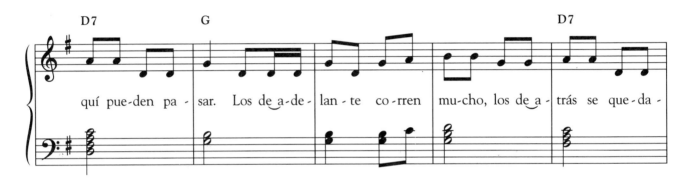

quí pue - den pa - sar. Los de_a - de - lan - te co - rren mu - cho, los de_a - trás se que - da -

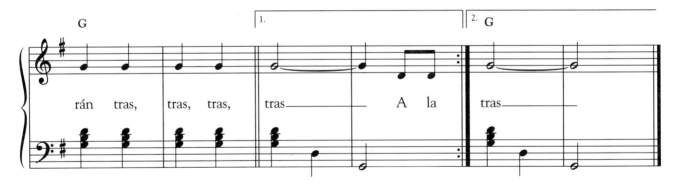

rán tras, tras, tras, tras——— A la tras———

A la víbora, víbora
de la mar, de la mar
por aquí pueden pasar.
Los de adelante corren mucho,
los de atrás se quedarán
tras, tras, tras, tras.

*The sea serpent we like to play
to have fun, to have fun
under the bridge all on track.
Children in front go faster and faster,
if you don't follow, you'll stay back,
back, back, back, back.*

La araña pequeñita · The Eensy, Weensy Spider

This finger-rhyme song is familiar to many children. The spider going up the water-spout is made by walking the hands, forefinger to thumb, upward. Wiggly fingers coming down make the rain, and vigorous arm gestures wash the spider out. An arm circle shows the sun, an expansive gesture dries out the rain, and the spider climbs again, forefinger to thumb. The great big spider is made with palms facing each other, one up, one down, and the arms moving apart, then together.

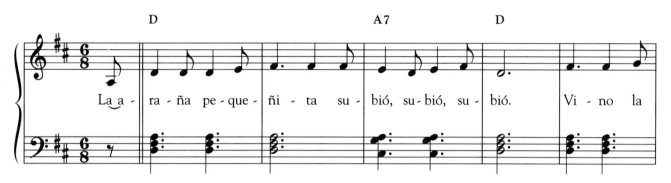

La a- ra-ña pe-que-ñi-ta su- bió, su-bió, su- bió. Vi - no la

llu - via y se la lle-vó. Sa - lió el sol y to-do lo se-

có, y la a- ra-ña pe-que-ñi - ta su- bió, su-bió, su-bió—

La araña pequeñita
subió, subió, subió.
Vino la lluvia
y se la llevó.
Salió el sol
y todo lo secó,
y la araña pequeñita
subió, subió, subió.

The eensy, weensy spider
went up the waterspout.
Down came the rain
and washed the spider out.
Out came the sun
and dried up all the rain,
and the eensy, weensy spider
went up the spout again.

La araña grandotota
subió, subió, subió.
Vino la lluvia
y se la llevó.
Salió el sol
y todo lo secó,
y la araña grandotota
subió, subió, subió.

The great big spider
went up the waterspout.
Down came the rain
and washed the spider out.
Out came the sun
and dried up all the rain,
and the great big spider
went up the spout again.

Las mañanitas · Special Morning Song

This is a traditional Mexican song that people sing early in the morning on birthdays or on other special days. Young men also serenade their girlfriends with this beautiful song. There are many mañanitas songs—this is only one of them.

(Lyrics on next page)

Estas son las mañanitas
que cantaba el rey David.
Hoy que es día de tu cumpleaños
te las cantamos así.

CORO
Despierta, mi bien, despierta,
mira que ya amaneció,
ya los pajarillos cantan,
la luna ya se metió.

Si el sereno de la esquina
me quisiera hacer favor
de apagar su linternita
mientras que pasa mi amor.

Despierta, mi bien…

Ahora sí, señor sereno,
le agradezco su favor,
prenda ya su linternita
que ya ha pasado mi amor.

Despierta, mi bien…

We are singing morning songs
as King David used to do.
Since today it is your birthday
we are here to sing them to you.

CHORUS
Awaken, my love, awaken,
and see that the day has dawned,
that the little birds are singing
and that the moon is long gone.

If the friendly corner watchman
might consent to be so kind
and put out his hanging lantern
as I watch my love pass by.

Awaken, my love…

It's all right now, Mr. Watchman,
thanks a lot for being so nice,
you may now relight your lantern,
my love already passed by.

Awaken, my love…

La villa · The Village

Here's a traditional chant a child can say when playfully taking over a seat that has
been vacated. Or the rhyme can be recited as a way of asking for a seat.

El que se fué a la villa
perdió su silla.

Move your feet,
lose your seat.

OR

Left my chair to go into town,
lost my chair, I can't sit down.

Compadre, cómpreme · Compadre, Buy Me
un coco · a Coconut

The word *compadre* is a term of honor denoting a man who is such a good friend that he is the godfather of his friend's child. This rhyme from the Dominican Republic uses that word to make a tricky tongue twister. It can be recited accompanied by finger snapping, clapping, or striking the thighs with the palms to keep the rhythm.

Com - pa - dre, cóm - pre - me un co - co, com -

pa - dre, no com - pro co - co___ por - que co - mo po - co co - co

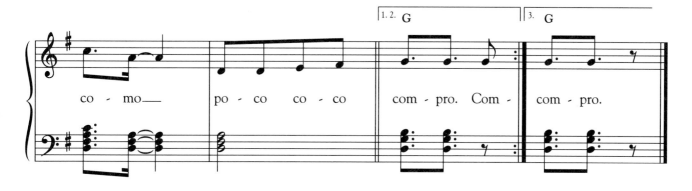

co - mo___ po - co co - co com - pro. Com - com - pro.

Compadre, cómpreme un coco,
compadre, no compro coco
porque como poco coco como,
poco coco compro. [cantar dos veces]

Compadre, buy me a coconut,
compadre, I don't buy coconut.
Since I eat very little coconut,
few coconuts I buy. [sing twice]

De colores · Bright with Colors

"De colores" came to the Americas from central Spain in the sixteenth century and is now sung all over the Spanish-speaking world on special occasions and celebrations. It is also the anthem of the United Farmworkers of America, a union founded by César Chávez, most of whose members are Spanish-speaking. People hold hands and sway while singing this beautiful song.

De_____ co - lo - res, de co - lo - res se vis - ten los

cam - pos en la pri - ma - ve - ra_____ De_____ co -

lo - res, de co - lo - res son los pa - ja - ri - tos que

vie - nen de a - fue - ra_____ De_____

(Lyrics on page 31)

De colores,
de colores se visten los campos
en la primavera.
De colores,
de colores son los pajaritos que vienen
de afuera.
De colores,
de colores es el arcoiris que vemos
lucir.

CORO
Y por eso los grandes amores
de muchos colores me gustan
a mí.   [cantar dos veces]

Canta el gallo,
canta el gallo con el kiri, kiri, kiri, kiri, kiri.
La gallina,
la gallina con el cara, cara, cara, cara, cara.
Los pollitos,
los pollitos con el pío, pío, pío, pío, pí.

CORO
Y por eso...

De colores,
bright with colors the mountains and valleys
dress up in the springtime.
De colores,
bright with colors all the little birds
fill the skies in the daytime.
De colores,
bright with colors the rainbow brings joy
with the glory of spring.

CHORUS
And a bright love with colors has found us
with peace all around us
that makes our hearts sing.   [sing twice]

Hear the rooster,
hear rooster singing kiri, kiri, kiri, kiri, kiri.
In the morning,
in the morning the hen sings her cara, cara, cara, cara, cara.
All day singing,
baby chicks all day sing pío, pío, pío, pío, pí.

CHORUS
And a bright love...

Los pollitos · The Baby Chicks

This Cuban version of "Los pollitos" makes a good game. For the first verse, one child represents the hen, and the rest of the children walk around the hen in a circle, moving their elbows up and down to imitate baby chicks. For the second verse, the circle stops moving and the hen walks around looking for food and feeding the chicks. For the third, the chicks sit down and close their eyes to rest, while the hen walks around giving them comfort.

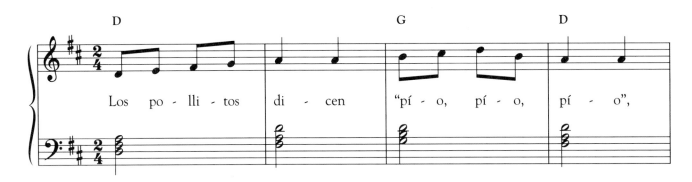

Los po - lli - tos di - cen "pí - o, pí - o, pí - o",

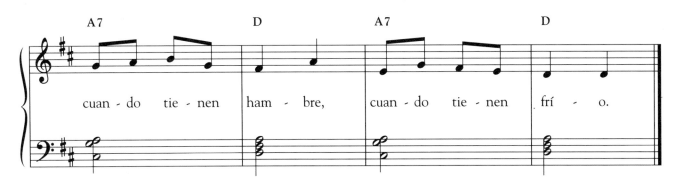

cuan - do tie - nen ham - bre, cuan - do tie - nen frí - o.

Los pollitos dicen	*Baby chicks are singing*
"pío, pío, pío",	*"pío, pío, pío,"*
cuando tienen hambre,	*"mamma we are hungry,"*
cuando tienen frío.	*"mamma we are cold."*
La gallina busca	*Mamma looks for wheat,*
el maíz y el trigo,	*mamma looks for corn,*
les da la comida	*mamma feeds them dinner,*
y les presta abrigo.	*mamma keeps them warm.*
Bajo sus dos alas	*Under mamma's wings*
acurrucaditos	*sleeping in the hay*
hasta el otro día	*baby chicks all huddle*
duermen los pollitos.	*until the next day.*

Las hormiguitas · The Little Ants

José-Luis Orozco wrote this rhyme in California. It can be played as a lively follow-the-leader game. In a line, children follow a leader, who makes up movements to the verses of the song. Children can take turns being the leader every other verse or so.

Por los ce-rri-tos_____ y ve-re-di-tas_____ van ca-mi-nan-do_____ las hor-mi-gui-tas_____

Por los cerritos	Over the little hills
y vereditas	and all the little roads
van caminando	the line of little ants
las hormiguitas.	**walk on and on.**

Las hormiguitas,	The line of little ants,
las hormiguitas,	the line of little ants,
van caminando	the line of little ants
las hormiguitas.	**walk on and on.**

Repeat the song, each time replacing the words in boldface with one of the phrases below.

van de puntitas	walk on tippy-toes
van dando vueltas	spin on and on
saltan y saltan	jump on and on
bailan y bailan	dance on and on
van patinando	skate on and on
ya se despiden	all wave good-bye

Las hormiguitas · 33

Sana, sana · Sana, Sana

This rhyme has magical healing power. Gently rub your fingers over a cut, bruise, or other injury in a circular motion, reciting the rhyme several times. The injured person will quickly feel better. "Sana, sana" means "heal, heal." This version comes from Ecuador. Use the rhythm below when reciting "Sana, sana."

Sa - na, sa - na co - li - ta de ra - na, si no sa - nas hoy sa - na - rás ma - ña - na.

Sana, sana
colita de rana,
si no sanas hoy
sanarás mañana.

Sana, sana
frog tail is in sorrow.
If I rub today
you'll be healed tomorrow.

Un ratoncito · A Little Mouse

This is a traditional rhyme. Walk your forefinger and middle finger over your opposite arm—or someone else's arm—from hand to elbow. This is un ratoncito, "a little mouse." Clap once before you say the last line.

Un ratoncito
iba por un arado
y este cuentecito
ya se ha acabado.

A little mouse ran
to swim in a pond
and this little story
is now long gone.

Cuatro camaroncitos · Four Little Shrimp

This nonsense song from Nicaragua can be acted out by children any way they like. They can pretend to be swimming underwater, or serving coffee, or whatever they wish.

A - llá en los ma - res don - de yo es - tu - ve den - tro del a - gua cer - ca de un mes ___ ha-bía u-nos pe - ces tan chi-qui - ti - tos co-mo la pun - ta de un al - fi - ler. Cua - tro ca - ma - ron - ci - tos me da - ban de co - mer ___ y u - na sar - di - na gran - de me ser - ví - a el ca - fé.

Allá en los mares
donde yo estuve
dentro del agua
cerca de un mes,
había unos peces
tan chiquititos
como la punta
de un alfiler.

There in the ocean
where I was living
under the water
close to a month,
the fish were tiny
so very tiny
just like the point
of a little pin.

Cuatro camaroncitos
me daban de comer,
y una sardina grande
me servía el café.

Four teeny-weeny-wee shrimp
fed me all dressed in pink,
and a humongous sardine
was serving coffee to drink.

¡Ay! cómo me quemaba,
agua por Dios pedía,
y un camarón me dijo,
"Eso sí que no hay aquí".

Oh boy the coffee was hot!
Water for burns I ordered,
and the silly shrimp responded,
"Sorry there's no water here."

El burrito enfermo · The Sick Little Donkey

This cumulative song is popular all over Latin America. Singers can alternate clapping their hands with stamping their feet at the "tap, tap, tap, tap" end of every verse. In English, you can also add the word "Hooray!" Children can point to the different parts of their bodies and pretend to put on the clothing mentioned in the song. Or one child can be the sick little donkey, and others can take turns bringing the donkey remedies.

A mi bu-rro, a mi bu-rro le due-le la ca-be-za, y el

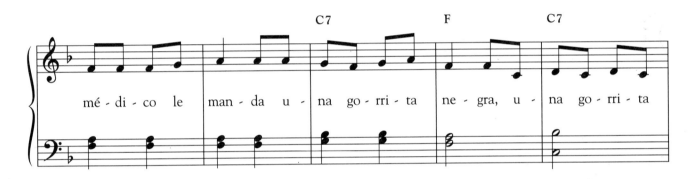

mé-di-co le man-da u-na go-rri-ta ne-gra, u-na go-rri-ta

ne-gra y mue-ve las pa-ti-tas tap, tap, tap, tap.

A mi burro, a mi burro
le duele la cabeza,
y el médico le manda
una gorrita negra,
una gorrita negra
y mueve las patitas
tap, tap, tap, tap.

My donkey has a headache,
my donkey cannot play,
the vet will soon deliver
a black hat and some hay,
a black hat and some hay,
and click your little hooves
tap, tap, tap, tap. Hooray!

(Lyrics continued on next page)

A mi burro, a mi burro
le duele la garganta,
y el médico le manda
una bufanda blanca,
una bufanda blanca,
una gorrita negra
y mueve las patitas
tap, tap, tap, tap.

My donkey has a sore throat,
my donkey cannot play,
the vet will soon deliver
a white scarf and some hay,
a white scarf and some hay,
a black hat for the headache,
and click your little hooves
tap, tap, tap, tap. Hooray!

A mi burro, a mi burro
le duelen las costillas,
y el médico le manda
chaqueta amarilla,
chaqueta amarilla,
una bufanda blanca,
una gorrita negra
y mueve las patitas
tap, tap, tap, tap.

My donkey's ribs are very sore,
my donkey cannot play,
the vet will soon deliver
a yellow coat and hay,
a yellow coat and hay,
a white scarf for the sore throat,
a black hat for the headache,
and click your little hooves
tap, tap, tap, tap. Hooray!

A mi burro, a mi burro
le duele el corazón,
y el médico le manda
gotitas de limón,
gotitas de limón,
chaqueta amarilla,
una bufanda blanca,
una gorrita negra
y mueve las patitas
tap, tap, tap, tap.

My donkey's heart is aching,
my donkey cannot play,
the vet will soon deliver
lemon drops and hay,
lemon drops and hay,
a yellow coat for sore ribs,
a white scarf for the sore throat,
a black hat for the headache,
and click your little hooves
tap, tap, tap, tap. Hooray!

A mi burro, a mi burro
ya no le duele nada,
y el médico le manda
trocitos de manzana,
trocitos de manzana,
gotitas de limón,
chaqueta amarilla,
una bufanda blanca,
una gorrita negra
y mueve las patitas
tap, tap, tap, tap.

My donkey is very happy,
my donkey can now play,
the vet will soon deliver
green apples and some hay,
green apples and some hay,
lemon drops for heartache,
a yellow coat for sore ribs,
a white scarf for the sore throat,
a black hat for the headache,
and click your little hooves
tap, tap, tap, tap. Hooray!

Caballito blanco · My Little White Horse

This version of "Caballito blanco" comes from Chile. Singing this song, children can pretend to ride horses (or use brooms or sticks as horses), clicking their tongues before and after the song in a trotting rhythm.

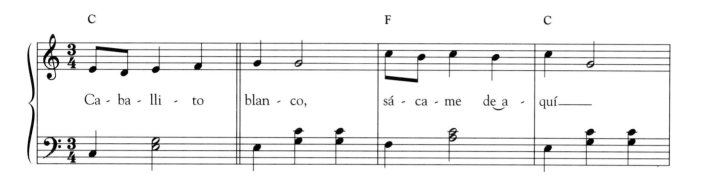

Caballito blanco,
sácame de aquí,
llévame a mi pueblo
donde yo nací.

Tengo, tengo, tengo,
tú no tienes nada,
tengo tres ovejas
en una cabaña.

Una me da leche,
otra me da lana,
y otra mantequilla
para la semana.

My little white horse,
take me now to my home,
take me to the nice town
where I was born.

I am very glad,
I am very lucky,
for I have three lambs
that make me so happy.

One lamb gives me wool,
one lamb gives me milk,
one lamb gives me butter
every single week.

La piñata · The Piñata

These are only a few of the many verses from two traditional Mexican songs that are sung during special celebrations like Christmas, Las Posadas, or school and birthday parties. A piñata is a clay pot or papier-mâché figure covered with colorful paper and filled with sweets and/or toys. A child is usually blindfolded and given a stick with which to try to break the piñata and spill out the goodies inside. Everybody shares the presents and helps clean up afterward!

An - da - le a - mi - go, no te di - la - tes con la ca - nas - ta de los ca - ca - hua - tes. An - da - le a - ci - ón.

Da - le, da - le, da - le, no pier - das el ti - no, mi - de la dis - tan - cia que hay en el ca - mi - no.

Andale amigo, no te dilates
con la canasta de los cacahuates.

Andale amigo, sal del rincón
con la canasta de la colación.

No quiero oro, ni quiero plata,
yo lo que quiero es romper la piñata.

Dale, dale, dale,
no pierdas el tino,
**mide la distancia
que hay en el camino.**

Repeat the last stanza, substituting the following lines for the last two lines in boldface.

porque si lo pierdes
pierdes el camino.

*Bring the piñata with no delay,
we want to party, we want to play.*

*Come on my friend, please don't be tardy,
bring us the baskets with all the candy.*

*I don't want silver, gold doesn't matter,
all that I want is to break the piñata.*

*Hit, hit the piñata,
do not lose your aim,
**measure well the distance
or you'll lose the way.***

*because if you lose it
you will lose the way.*

Nochebuena · Christmas Eve

"Nochebuena" is a Mexican song that celebrates Christmas Eve. The buñuelos mentioned in the song are Mexican pastries that are made of flour dough, deep fried, then covered with honey or syrup and sprinkled with cinnamon powder. Mmm…delicious!

Esta noche es Nochebuena,
noche de comer buñuelos,
noche de luna,
noche de estrellas
para los niños buenos.

Tonight is Christmas Eve,
a good night to eat buñuelos,
night with a big moon,
night with bright stars,
night for all the children.

Esta noche es Nochebuena,
noche de comer buñuelos,
noche de luna,
noche de estrellas
para las niñas buenas.

Tonight is Christmas Eve,
a good night to eat buñuelos,
night with a big moon,
night with bright stars,
night for all the children.

Nanita, nana · Nanita, Nana

"Nanita, nana" is sung at Christmastime in many Spanish-speaking countries. It's also sung as a lullaby. "Nanita" is an affectionate way of referring to a "nana," a baby-sitter or nanny.

A la na-ni-ta, na-na, na-ni-ta, na-na, na-ni-ta, e-a,

mi Je-sús tie-ne sue-ño, ben-di-to se-a, ben-di-to se-a.

Pa-ja-ri-llo que can-tas—— so—— bre el al-men-dro——

no des-pier-tes al ni-ño—— que es—— tá dur-mien-do——

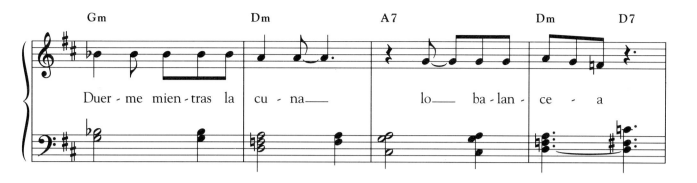

Duer - me mien - tras la cu - na___ lo ba - lan - ce - a

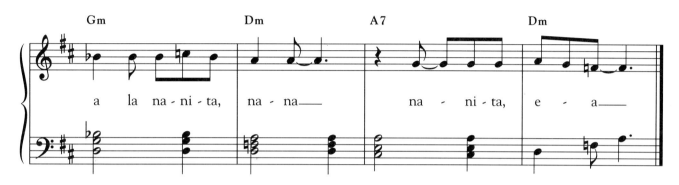

a la na - ni - ta, na - na___ na - ni - ta, e - a___

A la nanita, nana,
nanita, nana, nanita, ea,
mi Jesús tiene sueño,
bendito sea, bendito sea. *[cantar dos veces]*

Pajarillo que cantas
sobre el almendro,
no despiertes al niño
que está durmiendo.

Duerme mientras la cuna
lo balancea
a la nanita, nana,
nanita, ea.

Nana, nanita, nana,
nanita, nana, nanita, eh-a,
baby Jesus is sleeping,
blessings for him, nanita, eh-a. *[sing twice]*

Little bird that is singing
on the almond tree,
please don't wake up the baby,
he's soundly asleep.

He's sleeping while the cradle
rocks, to and fro,
nana, nanita, nana,
nanita, eh-a.

Naranja dulce · Sweet Orange

This farewell song is sung throughout Latin America. It can also be played as a game. For the first verse, children hold hands and walk around a child in the center of the circle. For the second verse, the circle stops moving and the center child picks another for handshaking and a farewell hug. For the third verse, the first child joins the circle, waving good-bye to the second child, who stays in the center. The game continues this way.

Na - ran - ja dul - ce, li - món par - ti - do, da - me un a -

bra - zo que yo te pi - do.

Naranja dulce,
limón partido,
dame un abrazo
que yo te pido.

Sweet honey orange,
a slice of lemon, dear,
if I could hug you,
if I could have you near.

Si fueran falsos
mis juramentos,
en otros tiempos
se olvidaran.

Time to shake hands now,
a hug for farewell,
Adiós amigo(a),
I wish you well.

Toca la marcha,
mi pecho llora,
adiós señora,
yo ya me voy.

The march is playing,
I'll part tomorrow,
Good-bye my dear friend,
I leave with sorrow.

El coquí · Coquí, the Little Frog

For many years a type of little frog in Puerto Rico has delighted children and grown-ups with its delightful song—"coquí, coquí." The sound has given the frog its name.

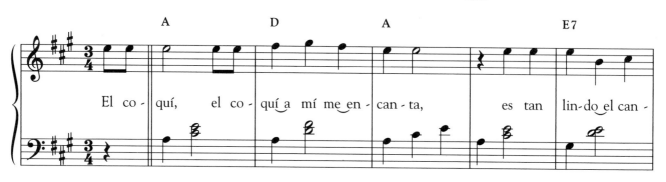

El co - quí, el co - quí a mí me en - can - ta, es tan lin-do el can -

tar del___ co - quí___ Por las no - ches al ir a a - cos -

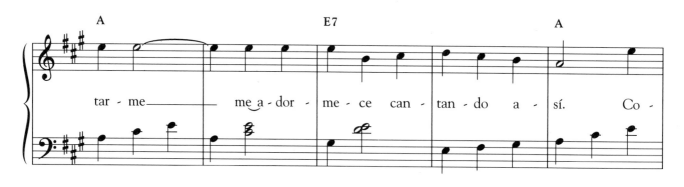

tar - me___ me a - dor - me - ce can - tan - do a - sí. Co -

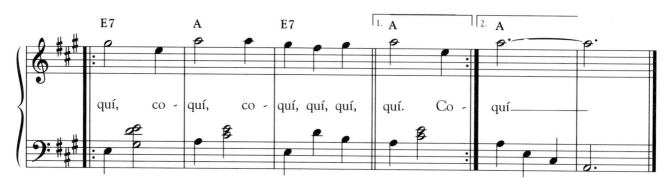

quí, co - quí, co - quí, quí, quí, quí. Co - quí___

El coquí, el coquí, a mí me encanta,
es tan lindo el cantar del coquí.
Por las noches al ir a acostarme,
me adormece cantando así.

Coquí, coquí, coquí, quí, quí, quí.
[*cantar dos veces*]

My *coquí, little frog, how I love you,*
for your songs give me comfort and peace.
Every night I can go to sleep happy
when I hear lullabies from coquí.

Coquí, coquí, coquí, quí, quí, quí.
[*sing twice*]

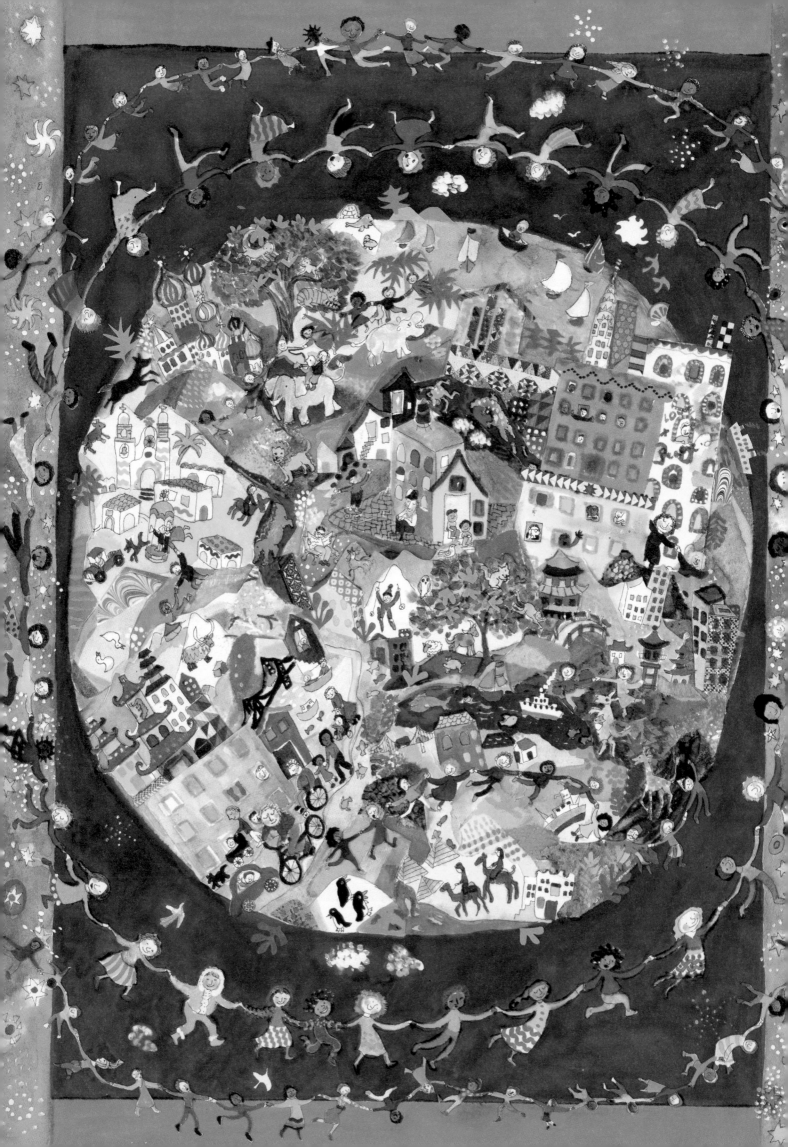

Paz y libertad · Peace and Liberty

This is an original song by José-Luis Orozco. It can be sung any time of the year, including Christmas. Children hold hands while they sing the song.

Lento

Pa - ra los ni - ños de to - do el mun - do que - re - mos paz y li - ber -

tad._____ Pa - ra los tad. Paz_____ que - re - mos paz

_____ y li - ber - tad_____ en es - te mun -

- do. - do. Ya no más ham -

Para los niños de todo el mundo queremos paz y libertad. [cantar dos veces]		For all the children in the world we want peace and liberty. [sing twice]
CORO Paz, queremos paz y libertad en este mundo. [cantar dos veces]		CHORUS Peace, we all want peace and liberty in this world. [sing twice]
Ya no más hambre, ya no más guerra, queremos paz en esta tierra. [dos veces]		No more hunger, no more war, we want peace on this earth. [twice]
Paz, queremos paz...		Peace, we all want peace...
Para los pobres y los viejitos queremos paz y libertad. [dos veces]		For the poor and the elderly we want peace and liberty. [twice]
Paz, queremos paz...		Peace, we all want peace...
Ya no más bombas ni radiación, no más ideas de exterminación. [dos veces]		No more bombs, no more radiation, no more ideas of extermination. [twice]
Paz, queremos paz...		Peace, we all want peace...

Duérmete, mi niño · Go to Sleep, My Baby

This lullaby originated in Spain and is sung throughout Latin America. For generations, mothers have used it to transmit love, warmth, and peace to their children as they fall asleep.

Duér-me-te, mi ni-ño, duér-me-te so-li-to,

que cuan-do des-pier-tes te da-ré a-to-li-to.

Duérmete, mi niño,	*Go to sleep, my baby,*
duérmete solito,	*sleep in peace and dream,*
que cuando despiertes	*for when you awaken*
te daré atolito.	*I will give you cream.*

Duérmete, mi niña,	*Go to sleep, my baby,*
duérmete, mi sol,	*go to sleep, my love,*
duérmete pedazo	*go to sleep, my sweetheart,*
de mi corazón.	*go to sleep, my dove.*

Subject Index